I Lost My Talk

Words by **Rita Joe**

Art by **Pauline Young**

NIMBUS
PUBLISHING
— NIMBUS.CA —

Nimbus Publishing Limited
3660 Strawberry Hill Street, Halifax, NS, B3K 5A9
(902) 455-4286 nimbus.ca

Printed and bound in Canada
NB1589

Design: Heather Bryan
Editor: Whitney Moran
Text on page 32 "About Rita Joe" adapted from *Amazing Atlantic Canadian Women*, © Stephanie Domet and Penelope Jackson, 2021, Nimbus Publishing

The publisher is grateful for the generosity of Breton Books for granting publication rights.

Library and Archives Canada Cataloguing in Publication
Title: I lost my talk / words by Rita Joe ; art by Pauline Young.
Names: Joe, Rita, 1932-2007, author. | Young, Pauline, 1965- illustrator.
Description: A poem.
Identifiers: Canadiana 20210128143 | ISBN 9781774710050 (softcover)
Classification: LCC PS8569.O265 I2 2021 | DDC C811/.54—dc23

Canadä   Canada Council   Conseil des arts   NOVA SCOTIA
             for the Arts   du Canada

Nimbus Publishing acknowledges the financial support for its publishing activities from the Government of Canada, the Canada Council for the Arts, and from the Province of Nova Scotia. We are pleased to work in partnership with the Province of Nova Scotia to develop and promote our creative industries for the benefit of all Nova Scotians.

I lost my talk

The talk you took away.

When I was a little girl
At Shubenacadie school.

angel   bo

You snatched it away:

I speak like you

I think like you

I create like you

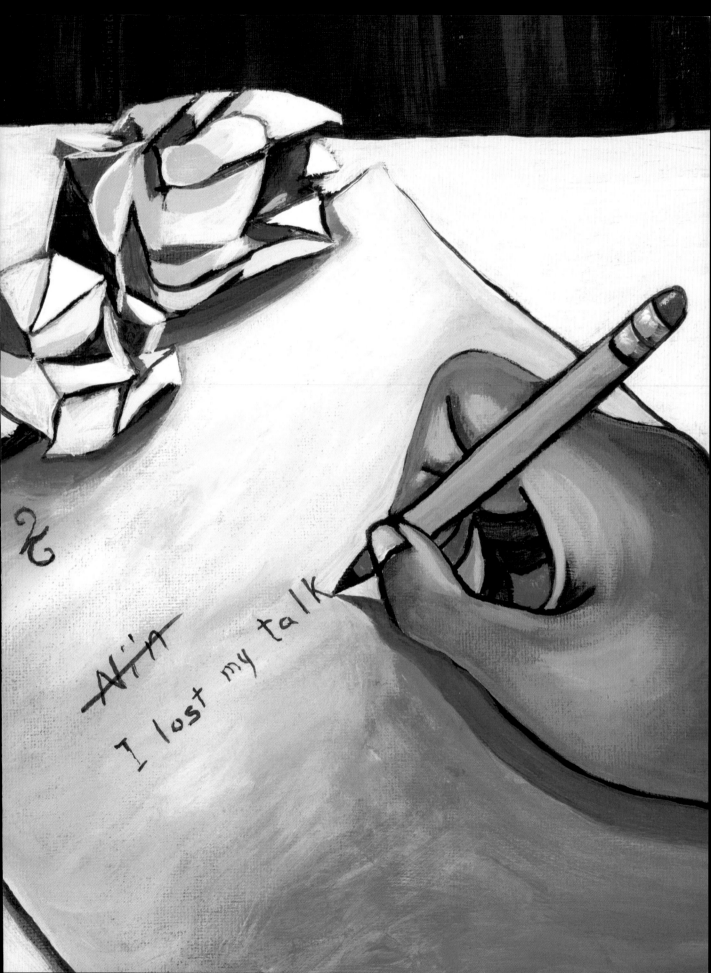

The scrambled ballad,
about my word.

Two ways I talk
Both ways I say,

Your way is more powerful.

So gently I offer
my hand and ask,

Let me find my talk

So I can teach you about me.

Children outside of the Shubenacadie School, c. 1930.

A Short History of Residential Schools

The Canadian government imposed its Indian Residential Schools program on Indigenous peoples for over one hundred years. It began in the 1870s and ended in 1996, when the final school, in Saskatchewan, was shut down.

Funded by the federal government and run by churches, who saw the residential school system as a chance to create new religious converts, these institutions were not really schools. They were an attempt by the Government of Canada to destroy Indigenous culture and peoples and eliminate what they called "the Indian problem." They were an attempt, the government admitted, to "take the Indian out of the child." To accomplish this goal, people known as Indian Agents, who worked for the newly created Department of Indian Affairs, would regularly snatch children from their communities. These children, sometimes as young as five, would typically remain at the schools until the age of sixteen.

Once imprisoned inside the schools, children were forbidden from speaking Indigenous languages, and physical and emotional abuse were often the punishment for speaking your mother tongue. Hair was cut short or shorn off completely, uniforms were enforced, and numbers replaced names. If a child did have a name, it was an English name given to them by the nuns who ran the schools. Much like

Europe's concentration camps during the Nazi regime in the Second World War, the effect was one of forced assimilation and dehumanization.

Instead of learning their own cultural ways and traditional knowledge, Indigenous children in residential schools suffered hard labour, were forced to spend long hours farming, cleaning, sewing, and even sometimes making crafts that the school would sell. This money did not go to the students, or to support their well-being.

Because the churches that ran the schools were paid more money the more students they had, the schools were often overcrowded. Diseases like tuberculosis were common, and many children suffered from malnutrition because they were not given proper food.

Children often died at the schools, for many reasons. They died from not receiving proper meals, from disease and illness, from accidents. Some died attempting to escape from these prisons; others committed suicide. Thirteen years before Shubenacadie opened, deaths at the schools were no longer being reported.

The Shubenacadie School, which Rita Joe attended and on which she based the poem "I Lost My Talk," was based in Shubenacadie, Nova Scotia. It opened in 1930 and operated for thirty-seven years as one of over 150 such schools across the country, attended in total by over 150,000 Indigenous children. During those years, the Shubenacadie School housed over 2,000 "students."

Rita Joe, like many others, left the school once she turned sixteen. At this age, children were typically sent away from residential school with no support, no family or community connections, and no money. They did not graduate; they survived.

In 1986 the shuttered Shubenacadie Residential School burned down in a suspicious fire. Many from the nearby Mi'kmaw reserve watched as flames consumed the building. Two days later, the building's remains were bulldozed, and all that was left was a dark and troubling legacy.

Rita Joe and her husband were both survivors of the Shubenacadie Residential School.

Source: Indian School Road: Legacies of the Shubenacadie Residential School *by Chris Benjamin.*

RON CAPLAN

About Rita Joe

Acclaimed poet Rita Joe (1932–2007) wrote seven books, won numerous awards, and continues to be an influence on poets and other artists across Canada.

Born in Whycocomagh, a Mi'kmaw reservation on Cape Breton Island, Nova Scotia, Joe, like many Indigenous children at the time, was sent to residential school. From the age of twelve to sixteen, she attended the Shubenacadie Residential School. She later moved to Boston before returning to Whycocomagh with her husband, Frank. Together, they raised ten children.

Perhaps her most famous poem, "I Lost My Talk" references Joe's time at Shubenacadie School, where she was forced, as per the brutal custom, to speak English instead of Mi'kmaw. She described having to re-learn her mother tongue by speaking with other Mi'kmaw people after leaving the school. "I Lost My Talk" inspired a multimedia performance at the National Arts Centre in 2016 as well as songs written by Indigenous youth across the country. This latter project especially would have probably pleased Joe, who wished more Indigenous people would become writers. She spoke at schools and encouraged children to write their own stories celebrating their culture. Rita Joe's poetry books *We Are the Dreamers*, *For the Children*, and *The Blind Man's Eyes* and her autobiography, *Song of Rita Joe*, are still in print and continue to be read and enjoyed by a whole new generation.